First published in 2020 by Laoch Publishing
22 Gowkhill Place, Larbert, Falkirk FK5 4US

Text copyright ©J.L.Bleakley 2020
Illustrations copyright © Shane Crampton 2020
Book design by Shane Crampton

ISBN: 978-1-8380849-1-2

For more information visit www.jlbleakley.com
Twitter: @JLBleakley

For my motley crew
Ian Lauryn and Kathryn

For Gran
Love Shane xxx

CHING SHIH

The Girl Who Ruled The Sea

Written by J.L.Bleakley

Illustrated by Shane Crampton

A girl looked out at the ocean,
Dreaming of what she could be,
Her head was full of adventure,
Her heart felt the call of the sea.

"Oh to leave these mountains behind,
And sail on the South China Sea.
Leading my very own pirate crew,
That is the life for me!"

"Don't be so silly," they told her,
"Girls can't be pirates," they said,

"It's safer on land, away from the shore,
Push those dreams out of your head."

Ching Shih would allow no such thing,
She knew what she had to do,
She used her brains and used her wits,
To arrange her very own crew.

Ching Shih looked out at the ocean,
From the helm of her ship, sailing free,

Her head was full of adventure,
Her heart sang the song of the sea.

"Oh to build this crew to a fleet,
The best on the South China Sea,

With thousands of men in my motley crew,
It's a pirate's life for me!"

"Don't be so silly," they told her,
"You'd never control them," they said,
"They'd turn against you and start a riot,
In a week you could lose your head!"

Ching Shih would allow no such thing,

She knew what she had to do,
She used her brains to make some rules,
A pirate code to lead her crew.

Ching Shih looked out at the ocean,
With her fleet, as wild as could be,
Her head was full of adventure,
Her heart sang the song of the sea.

"Oh to have mountains of treasure,
The richest on the South China Sea,
Our success would go down in legend,
It's the pirate's life for me!"

"Don't be so silly,"
they told her,
"You never could do it,"
they said,

"The pirates would fight
for each other's gold,
in a week you would all
be dead."

Ching Shih would allow no such thing,
She knew what she had to do,
She used her brains to share out the gold,
So each pirate got their fair due.

Ching Shih looked out at the ocean,
The greatest pirate in all history,
Her head was full of adventure,
Her heart sighed the song of the sea.

"Oh to start the next chapter,
To find peace on the South China Sea,
We're famous and rich, but feel empty,
I want more than this life for me."

"Don't be so silly," they told her, "You never could do it," they said,

"The Chinese Emperor is after you, He'll catch you and chop off your head."

WANTED
懸賞

Ching Shih would allow no such thing,
She knew what she had to do,

She used her brains to work
out a deal, to win freedom
for her and her crew.

Ching Shih looked out at the ocean,
Thinking of all she'd achieved,
Now her arms were full of adventure,
Singing her baby the song of the sea.

"Long ago I left these mountains behind,
I conquered the South China Sea,
Now I'm back with my own little crew,
I know this is the life for me."

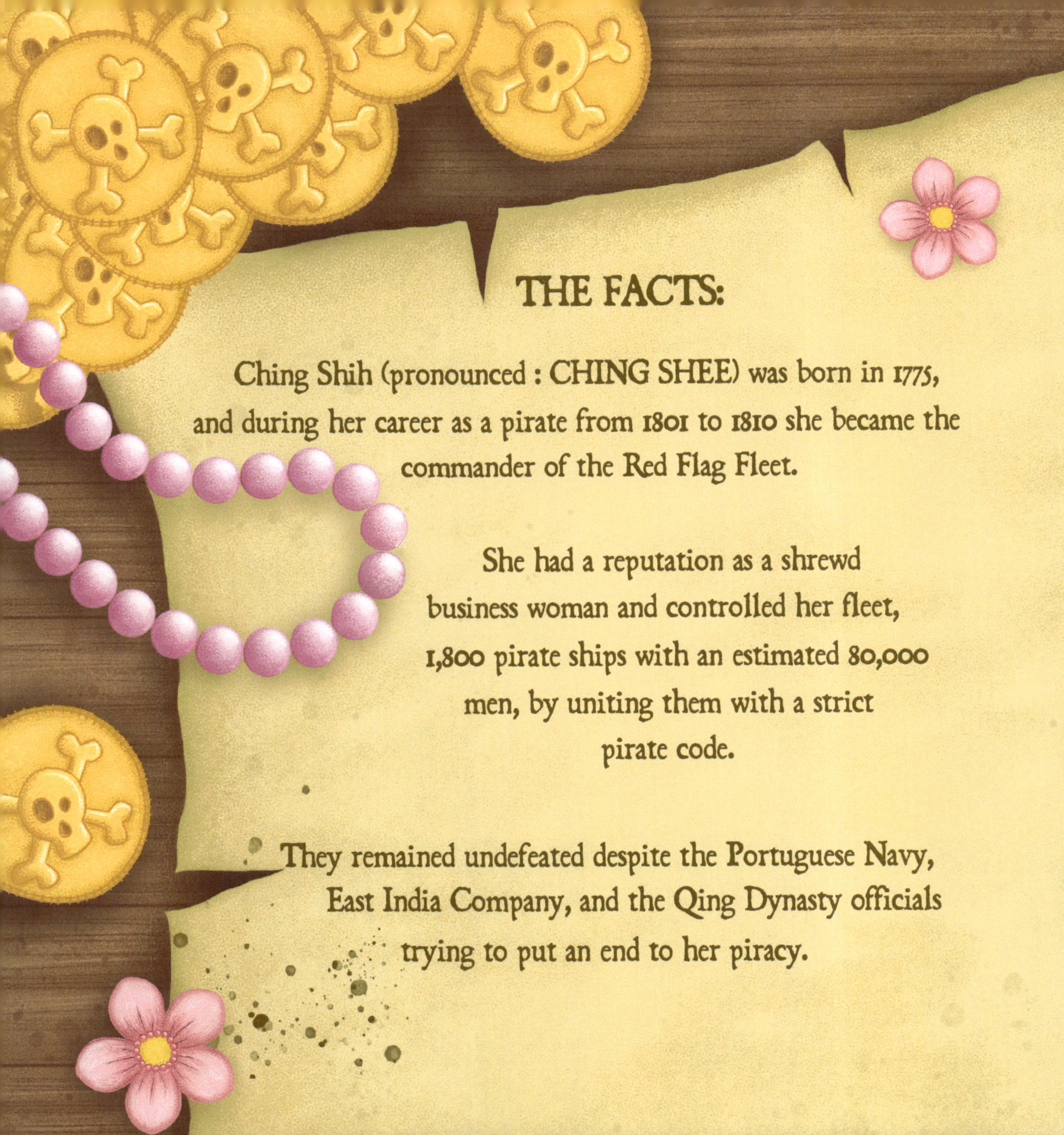

THE FACTS:

Ching Shih (pronounced : CHING SHEE) was born in 1775, and during her career as a pirate from 1801 to 1810 she became the commander of the Red Flag Fleet.

She had a reputation as a shrewd business woman and controlled her fleet, 1,800 pirate ships with an estimated 80,000 men, by uniting them with a strict pirate code.

They remained undefeated despite the Portuguese Navy, East India Company, and the Qing Dynasty officials trying to put an end to her piracy.

Finally, in 1810, she negotiated a
deal with the Chinese Emperor that
granted her complete amnesty and
allowed her to keep all her treasure and power,

making her the most successful pirate of all time.

She settled down and
had a family and lived to the
age of 69.